I Hit the Ball!

BASEBALL POEMS FOR THE YOUNG

ALSO BY GENE FEHLER

Center Field Grasses: Poems from Baseball
(McFarland, 1991)

I Hit the Ball!

BASEBALL POEMS FOR THE YOUNG

by Gene Fehler

McFarland & Company, Inc., Publishers
Jefferson, North Carolina, and London

Cover photo: "Baseball Brothers," by Cynthia Dufour Leslie; used by permission

Illustrations: Mike Schacht

The author gratefully acknowledges the following publications, in which some of the poems have appeared: *Capper's, Elysian Fields Quarterly, Faith 'n Stuff, Hob-Nob, Voices International.*

British Library Cataloguing-in-Publication data available

Library of Congress Cataloguing-in-Publication data available

ISBN 0-7864-0232-6 (sewn softcover; 55# alk. paper)

©1996 Gene Fehler. All rights reserved

No part of this book may be reproduced or transmitted in any form or by any means, electronic or mechanical, including photocopying or recording, or by any information storage and retrieval system, without permission in writing from the publisher.

Manufactured in the United States of America

McFarland & Company, Inc., Publishers
  Box 611, Jefferson, North Carolina 28640

With love and thanks
to Polly,
Andy and Misty,
Tim and Jacquelyn —

Nothing important in my life ever gets done
without their love and support.

Contents

Preface	viii
PART ONE	
The Strange World of Baseball	1
PART TWO	
Fans, Families and Bench-Warmers	23
PART THREE	
Playing the Game	41
PART FOUR	
Baseball Dreams and Desires	63
PART FIVE	
A Player's Primer	81
With the Bat	83
On the Mound and On the Bases	92
With the Glove	102
Some Final Thoughts	111

Preface

As long as our world has children, baseball will never die.

Children understand, perhaps intuitively, the beauty of baseball — the thrill of taking a broomstick or a piece of wood or an aluminum bat and trying to make contact with a thrown missile, perhaps a regulation ball, but maybe some wadded tape or a ping-pong ball or a rubber ball the size of a marble.

And, oh, the magic when the two meet, often sending into motion still a third child, measuring speed and distance and angle, thrusting out a hand — bare or gloved — to try to trap the missile and put the batter out.

Baseball games on real fields and imaginary fields, played with standard rules and made-up rules by all-stars and the boy or girl still waiting for that first hit or the first crucial catch, will always hold strong memories for millions of grown-up children.

Such are the stuff of baseball dreams, the dreams of children of all ages. Such are the dreams that poems are made from.

GENE FEHLER
April, 1996

Part One

The Strange World of Baseball

The Rules of Baseball?

I remember all the rules
    Of how to play the game.
A team gets four outs each at bat,
    And eight outs make a frame.

Ten frames in all make up a match.
    Three matches make a set.
Are you surprised I know the rules?
    You thought I would forget.

Five strikes will walk a batter.
    Six balls, the batter fans.
It's called a home run when a foul ball
    Goes into the stands.

In touching all the bases,
    You have to use both feet.
The umps will watch you closely
    To see that you don't cheat.

I love the rules of baseball.
    They make it fun to play.
And I work hard to learn at least
    One new rule each day.

Playing Ball in the Churchyard

I smashed one toward the window —
   Smashed glass, expensive, new.
Harmlessly, the ball bounced off
   Instead of going through.

I breathed a sigh of great relief
   And raised my eyes to see
If God's gloved hand had darted down,
   Protecting glass and me.

Window Noises

I always hate
   To hear the sound
   Of windows when
I'm playing ball.

I've noticed that
   Unless it breaks,
   The window makes
No sound at all.

What If?

...You could get the runner out
by hitting him with a thrown ball?

...The umpire wasn't behind the catcher,
but sitting on a chair down the first base line?

...The catcher and all the fielders
caught every ball with their bare hands?

...It took nine called "balls" before
a hitter could be walked?

...The pitcher could take several steps forward
before releasing the pitch?

...The batter was out if the fielder caught a
batted ball on one bounce?

...A batter could get a hit even on a ball
hit outside the foul lines?

...The bases were wooden stakes projecting
four feet from the ground?

Why, you'd be playing by some of the rules
of baseball from way back in the 1800s.

A Field of Pitcher's Mounds

The field where we play our home games
has eight pitcher's mounds,
one in front of every fielder.

No one can know for sure which direction
a ground ball will bounce.

Sometimes fielders charge a grounder
and take a crazy bounce off a mound themselves.

Mountain climbers make the best base stealers.

Our third baseman is so short
our catcher can see just the top of his head.

Our pitcher doesn't have an advantage
because the batter stands on a mound too,
and our catcher has a hard time
catching any pitch above the batter's knees.

Outfielders sometimes stand on top of the mound
so all they have to do is run down it
when the ball is hit, and they can get
their legs moving pretty fast.

I bet you can hardly wait to come play us on our field.

Handles on Baseballs?

The part that is called *the handle*
   Is the slender part of the bat.
But what if balls had handles, too?
   Just how would you feel about that?

Just picture a handle on baseballs
   That you have to catch or throw.
And if you should hit on the handle
   How far do you think it would go?

Put handles on baseballs? Not likely.
   The idea's not very sound.
The handles of bats should be slender,
   And baseballs — well, they should be round.

Big, Hungry Gloves

Back in baseball's
early years

fielders wore
no gloves at all.

But gloves today
are big enough

to swallow whole
a basketball.

Losing in the Big Leagues Because of a Bad Hop

Sometimes
a pebble
is all
that's
required
for an unlucky
coach
to end up
fired.

Southpaw

I'm what they call a southpaw:
   I throw with my left hand.
Why righties aren't called northpaws
   I'll never understand.

Schoolyard Monkeybars

I sit on schoolyard monkeybars
   And drop my baseball toward an ant.
I wonder if the ant can catch it.
   Whoops! I just found out it can't.

Undersea Baseball: The Octopus

Five coaches couldn't quite agree
   On where the octopus should play.
One saw him as a pitching star:
   "He'll have a fresh arm every day."

One said, "First base. Eight tentacles
   Could snag up every wild throw."
One wanted him behind the plate,
   "To block those pitches, high and low."

Another urged, "Put him at short.
   He's worth four Ripkins," that coach said.
A fifth coach wanted him to roam
   The center field seas instead.

He wound up sitting on the bench
   As all five coaches' right hand man.
And left. and right. and left. and right.
   And left. and right. and left again.

I Memorized the Ball

I memorized the ball so well
I could see every stitch
from the moment it left
the pitcher's long skinny fingers
and rotated toward me, spinning
faster than the earth itself.

I memorized the ball so well
I could read every word written on it.
The name of the league president
spoke to me, saying, "How do you do?"
"Fine," I said, and I hit the ball
smack on his name and memorized it
all the way over the fence.

The only thing is, the next time
the pitcher threw me the same pitch,
I forgot to remember
where it was supposed to go,
and the catcher memorized it
right into his big mitt.

Mouth of the Infield

When the season ends
Coach yanks the bases out
like decayed teeth
and the infield
gums its goodbye
like an old woman
who knows her next
dentist appointment
is still six months away
and all she can eat
is the soft snow of winter.

Monster of the Mound

I am the monster of the mound,
    I snort and stomp and throw.
And no one knows, not even me,
    Just where the pitch will go.

I am the monster of the mound;
    But there's one thing I hate:
An even bigger, meaner monster's
    Batting at home plate.

I Wrote a Poem with My Baseball Bat

I wrote a poem with my baseball bat.
It was only four lines long
And it didn't even rhyme,
But it was a great poem.

The first line was "Touched first base."
Line two was "Touched second base."
The third line was "Touched third base."
The last line was "Touched home plate."
The title that my bat gave the poem
Was **HOME RUN.**

It was the best poem my bat and I ever wrote.

The Longest Hit

The longest hit I've ever seen
Was made last night by Billy Green.

He hit a fast ball with such power
It sailed above our water tower.

It traveled so far through the night
It barely missed a satellite

And kept on going toward the moon.
It's still not back this afternoon.

Standing on My Head to Play Baseball

When I stand on my head
to play the outfield,
fly balls do not exist
and the grass tickles my nose.

When I stand on my head to pitch,
my sinker rises
above the batter's eyes
and I catch line drives with my feet.

When I stand on my head to bat
and the umpire
stands on his head to call pitches,
the catcher does not know
where the strike zone is
and anything under the fence
is a home run.

Superstitious Teammates

Mary chews fresh bubble gum
In every other inning.
Bobby wears long underwear
As long as we keep winning.

Before each time at bat, Miguel
Rubs dirt on both his knees.
Coach says a prayer when Terry hits,
Looks skyward, and begs, "Please."

Joseph turns a somersault
Each inning at first base.
Before each curve that Sara throws
She makes a funny face.

Well, I'm not superstitious —
Not even just a bit.
But now I'd better kiss my bat:
It's almost time to hit.

The Wall, Watching a Home Run

It wishes
it could leap
to stop
that long fly
ball,

But, oh
alas,
it cannot
move at all,

that lifeless
unfielding
wooden
outfield wall.

Two No-Hitters in One Year

Four pitchers tossed two no-hit games
   In just a single year:
Allie Reynolds, Virgil Trucks,
   And Johnny Vandermeer.

That's only three, so in this verse
   The best is saved for last:
Who else but Nolan Ryan, who
   They say was kind of fast.

Batting Helmets on My Brain

I'm glad that we wear them for batting
    And running the bases, too.
I've seen a few scatter-armed players
    Whose aim was not very true.

A ball bopped me once in a ballgame,
    But happily I felt no pain.
I'm glad I had all that strong plastic
    Protecting my marvelous brain.

My Big Left Toe

Inside my sock it yells in pain,
    My big left toe.
It happens when a wild pitch
    Breaks in and low.

Inside my sock my big left toe
    Grows red and fat.
It likes it better when I field
    Than when I bat.

Drought or Deluge?

I'm pitching today
in the midst
of a drought.

My friend Tom
says
dry ice
sprinkled into clouds
will bring rain.

He says if
the same is true
of baseballs
sprinkled into clouds
we'll soon
have a deluge

with me
pitching
today.

The Most Amazing Play

The most amazing play I've seen
    Happened just last night.
A fly ball high into the dome
    Struck and broke a light.

Some jagged glass cut through the ball
    And sliced it right in two.
The center fielder got both halves,
    Picked them up, and threw.

The fans let out the biggest roar
    I think I've ever heard:
The pieces threw two runners out—
    At second and at third.

My Dog's Feast

My dog chewed up my ball,
    My only one.

He nibbled numbers off
    My baseball shirt.

And then he brought to me
    My catcher's mitt—

At least what still remained
    Of his dessert.

What Did the Ball Say?

What did the ball say to the mitt?
  "I think we'd make a perfect fit."

What did the leg say to the bag?
  "Help me to avoid the tag."

What did the chalk say to the line?
  "Keep going straight, we're doing fine."

What did the coach's sign say to the batter?
  "You missed another one. What's the matter?"

What did the bat say to the ball?
  "I don't want to miss you;
  I'd much rather kiss you."

What did the catcher say to the mask?
  "Am I good-looking?"
          "Don't even ask."

All Through the Game

All through the game
the hits went hopping
past the infielders,
never stopping or even
pausing to say "Hello,"
or "Ha, you missed me!"

All through the game
the flies kept falling
out of reach of stumbling
outfielders reaching,
calling, "Mine, no yours!"
"I got it ... no I don't."

All through the game
the fans would rise
to laugh and cheer each
magic out as if the one
who caught the ball was
some big leaguer in disguise.

All through the game
the runs kept scoring,
and when the game
was finally over
(43 to 41), we all agreed:
it wasn't boring!

Solar System Baseball

If there's baseball on the moon
do they play night games
beneath a full earth?

If there's baseball on the sun
where do they go to find shade?

If there's baseball on Pluto
are games interrupted
by barking dogs?

If there's baseball on Mercury
are outfield grasses red?

If there's baseball on Saturn
do people from Mars
and Jupiter and Uranus
park their space ships
on the rings and watch?

If there's baseball
in other solar systems
do they measure innings
by light years
and use stars for baseballs?

Part Two

Fans, Families and Bench-Warmers

At Dad's Softball Game

The summer before fourth grade
Dad took me to his softball game,
fifteen miles from home.
"We'll be back by nine," he told Mom.
He let me sit in the dugout,
run out to pick up bats,
make sure our first baseman
got a warm-up ball each inning.
I lasted until the fourteenth inning,
then curled into sleep at the end of the bench,
learned later that our catcher Tommy Willis
covered me with his jacket,
that Dad carried me still sleeping to our car
behind the bleachers back of first base
in the eighteenth, checked on me
between every inning until the twenty-seventh,
when Tommy's home run won it
and we drove home to Mom after midnight
frantic next to a phone that never rang.

Catch with Gramps

Gramps pitched in the majors
before I was born,
led the league in walks twice.

Now in our backyard
he wears his old mitt,
barely larger than his hand.

He spits in its shiny pocket,

rubs the ball around,
floats the ball toward me

again and again,
tells me before each pitch
to hold my glove still.

And if he throws one straight,
I will.

Dad Hits Pop-ups

Dad hits pop-ups
so high that airplanes
make U-turns in the sky
and birds dive for cover
whenever they see
Dad in the backyard
with a bat in his hands
and a silly grin
on his face.

My Daddy Was a Player

My Daddy played the infield:
   Second, short, and third.
And man, he sure could play the game!
   At least that's what I've heard.

But whether it is true or not
   I might not ever know,
'Cause Daddy is the only one
   Who's ever told me so.

Mommy, Daddy, Me

Daddy pitches, I swing;
   Mommy runs like the wind
To field the ball that I hit.

Oh, it feels so good,
   This game that we play, that
I don't ever want us to quit.

Measure That Head Size

I'm pretty much the best there is:
   I hit and run and throw
Harder, faster, stronger,
   Than anyone I know.

So I don't understand my coach;
   I think that he's a sap.
He says he'll bench me till I get
   A smaller baseball cap.

That Ump Makes Me So Mad!

That blind old ump behind the plate! —
    He's such a scary sight.
His eyes look like tomatoes;
    His teeth are long and white.

Just like a dragon, flames shoot out
    From both his ears and nose.
And he calls "strike" on everything
    The other pitcher throws

(Especially when I'm at bat,
    And oh, it makes me mad)!
But when he doesn't ump my games,
    I really love my dad.

I'm on My Way

    Yesterday I hit the ball!
        My mom and dad were there.
    Maybe someday they can even
        See me hit one fair.

My Brother Ben

My brother Ben can't do the things
   Good players do.

He cannot throw or catch as well
   As me and you.

And take a proper batting stance?
   He has no clue.

My mom says, "Don't expect so much.
   He's only two."

Some Moms

Some moms come late from work,
fix broccoli, yell because
you tracked mud on the carpet.

Some moms talk on telephones
all day, watch TV, stuff
themselves with candy or cookies.

My mom plays shortstop,
dives in the dirt, reads me boxscores
from the morning paper.

Sure, Dad

Dad says they knocked the covers off,
    Then taped the stringy ball.
They pounded nails in broken bats,
    Then used them, nails and all!

My dad can tell some whoppers,
    But I nod to be polite.
A taped-up ball! A nailed-up bat!
    Imagine such a sight!

Their Son, the Would-Be Star

At every game
   Ed's mom and dad
Cheer loudly
   And they clap and say:

"Our Ed's the best!"
   It's such a shame
Coach hardly ever
   Lets him play.

In the Dusk

Mama's call,
"Come on home,"
reaches me
from down the street
just as the ball
almost hidden
in the gray of dusk
falls into my waiting glove.

I love that time best of all —

twilight after a summer day
filled with ballgames

bats blazing in the sun
the thump of horsehide
and flashing leather

the sweet sad sound
of Mama's call,
"Come on home."

My Proud Parents

I see my parents in the stands.
   They stand and cheer
And clap their hands.

And whether I play good or bad
   They're proud of me —
My Mom and Dad.

Disabled Fan

She never played a game.
She never hit a ball.
She never ran to first
Or leaped against a wall
To make a circus catch.
Crowds never cheered for her.
Yet on the baseball field
Is where her heroes are.

Free Swingers

I can't help but wonder
   Just how the ground feels
Whenever a free swinger
   Swings from his heels.

I hear *ooh's* and *aah's*
   As the bat stirs up breezes;
I see sawdust drip
   From the bat that he squeezes.

The smart one just waits
   For the pitcher's mistakes,
And when he connects,
   Well, the whole ballpark shakes.

Ballpark Sounds

Listen to the sound
of bat and ball when they meet
at blinding speed.

Listen to the sound
of pick-off throws as the runner
takes his lead.

Listen to the hush
that falls before each sudden
clap of hands.

Listen to the sound
of peanut vendors calling
through the stands.

Listen to the sound
of peanut shells when they crunch
beneath your shoes.

Listen to the cries
from bleacher fans when they see
the home team lose.

From the Bleachers

The game
unfolds
before me

in greens and browns
   of grass and ground,
blue and white
   of sky and cloud

and in between
   running bodies,
   shouting bodies
   anxious bodies

beneath a ball
   dancing
         drifting

with a mind
of its own
and the sun
and breeze
        its partners

Late and Early

I was late for dinner sometimes,
waiting until the last out
in our pick-up games down the street,
ignoring calls of "dinner's ready,"
pretending not to hear,
coming home to cold potatoes
and colder stares.

I was late for bed sometimes,
waiting until after the last hint
of sunlight peeked over the trees
beyond the right field fence,
watching a black ball drop
from gray dusk for the last out,
coming home to sharp glances
at our living room clock,
to "you can't play ball in the dark."

Yet every birthday and Christmas
Mom and Dad awoke early
to give me in a brightly wrapped box
a new baseball
or mitt.

Ballpark Quartet

baseballs
sing base

bats sing
tenor

gloves sing
soprano

while in the
stands

I hum the
melody

Warming the Bench

When you
are sitting
on the bench,
support your team
with cheers.
For when you play,
their shouts will be
sweet music to
your ears.

Grandma Says

Grandma says that when Mom
was my age girls couldn't play
on teams, only boys could.

She says that the girls all sat
in the bleachers and cheered
for their boyfriends. She says

that my Dad played third base
and batted clean-up, but that
even though Mom couldn't play

on any team she could hit harder
than he could and she could run
faster and field better and throw

a ball longer and bunt the ball
so good it would stop right
where Mom wanted it to.

My Dad just smiles, and I wonder
what he means when he watches
me play third base and tells people,

"Yes, she's a chip off the old block!"

Part Three

Playing the Game

What a Batter Feels

I tremble as I stand at the plate
with knocking knees and fluttering
heart waiting for the pitch.
I struggle for air.

My hands gripping
the bat are clenched and white.

The pitcher throws.
I close my eyes and swing
where I hope the pitch might be.
My hands vibrate at the solid contact.

I start sprinting
and I watch the ball take flight.

My knees are like steel coils.
I breathe again. My hands cut the air.
My feet barely touch ground
as I round first base. I grin.

I hear cheering
as the ball sails out of sight.

Arms

At short, John's arm is like a gun.
    At third base, so is Frank's.
But I play second with an arm
    That people say
    Is filled with blanks.

The Biggest Bat

I grabbed the biggest, fattest bat
    And swung hard as I could.
And if I would have hit the ball,
    I would have hit it good!

Diving Catch

"Great diving catch!"
    my teammates cheered.
      But one thing I won't tell
        is that I didn't dive at all;
          I merely slipped and fell.

The Coach and the Strike Out

I drop my gaze to the ground.
I feel my shoulders slump,
and I drag my bat behind me
back toward the wooden bench,
back toward our fans cheering
for our next hitter to come through.

Coach meets me halfway,
pats me on the back.
"You did a good job up there,"
he says. "You took some good cuts.
That's what I like to see
in my hitters."
I look up into his smile.
I lift up my shoulders.
I turn to cheer for our new batter.

An Awful Sound

I hear
the umpire

hiss
strike

it feels like
a snake

circling my
wrist

but I'm well
rid of it

each time
I swing

and I get
a hit.

Fast Ball

The fast ball
comes;
I swing.
I blink.

It went
right *through*
my bat,
I think.

I Love Baseball

I love it when our coach calls out
    every starter's name.
I love it most when I find out
    I'm playing in the game.

I love it when the umpire shouts
    across the field, "Play ball!"
I love to stand out in the field
    and feel ten feet tall.

I love to hear my teammates chatter
    and I love to shout.
I love it when we get those tough
    opposing batters out.

I love it when I hit the ball
    and when I score a run.
I love just playing baseball, and
    I love it 'cause it's fun.

Why Wear Myself Out?

I sat down in the outfield
   And I leaned against the wall.
I watched our pitcher speed them in;
   The batters missed them all.

At last Coach spied me sitting
   And he got plenty sore.
He waved me off the field right then.
   I didn't know what for.

When batters never hit the ball,
   I cannot see the sense
In standing up when I can sit
   And rest against the fence.

Here's My Mitt, Where's the Ball?

My teammates gasped. They'd never seen
   A baseball mitt so large.
"A bushel basket," someone said,
   While others called it "Barge."

On high fly balls, the mitt's great size
   Was not much help at all.
That big old mitt could never judge
   The flight of any ball.

Trying to Catch a Fly Ball

The ball
drops from
a crowded sky
filled with sun
cloud
birds
chunks of blue

all falling,
fighting for
my attention,

but my glove
has room for only
one.

Glove and mind
reach out
to sort them all

until what's left
of crowded sky
is just the
ball.

Before the Pitch

The catcher crouches,
points two fingers down,
paints a target
with rounded mitt.

The batter signals time,
steps out,
beats bat against
muddy cleats.

The catcher lifts
his mask away
so he can
spit.

I'm Not the Best

I cannot run as fast as Paul
   Or throw as hard as Cole.
Bonnie's better catching flies.
   My pitching? No control.

I can't hit line drives like Dan can,
   Or long home runs like Lou.
I can't scoop up those grounders
   Like I see Bill Kenney do.

But though I'm not the best there is,
   No player hustles more.
Coach says that's most important
   When they total up the score.

It's How You Play, Not What You Wear

The other guys
   looked like a team;
      Their uniforms were new.

We wore old pants
   and mismatched shirts
      And lost, nineteen to two.

Slow Curve

Curving like a half moon,
it sweeps toward me.

My body leans back;
the ball bends and teases.

It misses my bat
whenever it pleases.

Dust Cloud
at Second Base

The infield
is
a dust storm
waiting
to happen

waiting for
me —
the wind —
to steal
second base.

Headfirst Slide

With my toboggan-body-headfirst-slide
   The only time that I've been hurt
Is when I dropped my head so far
   My chin plowed furrows in the dirt.

Perfect Fit

Oh,
the joy

my mitt
feels

each time
it

and a batted
ball

make a perfect
fit.

It Just Isn't Fair

When I'm
        in the field,

          the open spaces

              are vast

as range land,

            large enough

        for a thousand

          grazing

cattle.

When I'm at bat,
a thousand fielders
stand side by side
on a battlefield
smaller than a closet.

Reading the Pitcher

He chewed gum fast, he chewed gum slow;
And how he chewed let hitters know
The kind of pitch that he would throw.

Fast chewing, fastball's on its way.
Slow chewing, curve: let's make him pay!
It was a batter's holiday!

He learned too late that we all knew
Before each pitch what it would do.
He learned too late how not to chew.

My Pitching Lullaby

The ball
starts its lullaby
in my pitching
hand

sings
all the way
into the
muffled darkness

of the
catcher's
pillowed
mitt.

The Sky Waits

I race
through
the outfield
toward
where the sky

waits to throw
at me
the batter's
pop
fly.

Shortstop, Shortstop, Help Me!

Shortstop, shortstop, help me!
Be kind. Do not grin at me
when my slide ends
four feet short of the bag.
Don't slap me with the tag.
Instead of poking the ball
in my face,
let me stand up, then chase
me back toward first base.
You can catch me in a rundown.
Shortstop, shortstop, be kind.
Give me a chance.

Knuckleball

It floats.

It dips like pirate ships
caught on waves that toss it
up
and
down.

I wait and wait
and here it comes,
pulled by strings
this way
and that

where is it at?

I wait and wait
it nears the plate

and now
and *now*

my bat swings
under (maybe over)
it

too soon
or was the swing

too late?

Keeping Track of Who's Ahead

In golf the scoring is by strokes,
    In bowling it's by pins.
In many sports we add up points
    To let us know who wins.

But baseball scoring's different,
    And to me the greatest fun
Is when I slide across home plate
    And score the winning run.

Making Music

My fingers drum
the bat handle,
limber up,
play the scales,
prepare for
their own sweet
music:

a banjo bunt,
a saxophone single,
a dulcimer double,
a trumpeting triple,
a harp-sweet
horn-blowing
homer

while fans in
curtainless bleachers
roar,
stand
to demand
an
encore.

The Man in the Bleachers

There's a man in the bleachers
    Guys say is a scout
For some major league team.
    And I just made an out!

When that man in the bleachers
    Writes my name in a book
He'll say, "No, don't bother;
    He's not worth a look."

Oh, the pressure of playing
    For money or fame.
I think I'll ignore him
    And just play the game.

The Snow and the Heat

The pitcher's leg
kicks off the mountain,
the foot almost in my face.
An arm flings snow
from the mountain's peak.

From below, the heat from my bat
waits to meet the white storm,
to send snow back in a form
no one will recognize,
or catch.

There Are Fielders Awaiting

There are fielders awaiting
    Every ball I hit.
Long or short or soft or hard,
    They're always catching it.

I can hit one twenty miles
    And they'll take the Amtrak train
And be waiting there to catch it
    When the ball comes down again.

Why, I can hit the ball so well
    I ought to be a hero.
It's just those dumb old fielders' fault
    That I'm still batting zero.

Skinned Knees Aren't So Bad

A skinned knee
    And a bloody lip,
A scratched-up face —
    All earned with pride.

Oh, sure, they hurt,
    But that's all right;
I made a headfirst
    Scoring slide.

On Second Street

On Second Street
our field of play
changes almost every day.

A car that marked first base
is gone, and in its place
a lidless garbage can
awaits the truck.
(With luck, a line drive
won't knock it over.)
We use its lid for second;
third is the hydrant.
From atop a sewer cover
our pitcher throws
the sweetest pitches.

Who could want more
from a field than this:
bases to race to,
a stick, a ball,
and us at play
all day
on Second Street.

Our Slowball Pitcher

Our pitcher winds up, throws the 3–2 pitch.
Behind the plate, I watch it float toward me.

I set my catcher's mitt on the ground,
slide a *Baseball Digest* from my back pocket,
and read an article about Nolan Ryan.

The ump pulls a harmonica from under his hat
and plays "Slow Boat to China."

The batter falls asleep waiting for the ball to arrive.

When it finally does there's nothing
for me to do except close my magazine,
pick up my mitt and hold it open for the ball.

And there's nothing for the batter to do
except dream of how he might have clobbered
that pitch had he stayed awake.

And there's nothing for the ump to do
but pause in the middle of the final chorus
to shout, "Strike Three!"

And there's nothing for our pitcher to do
except let his lips curve ever so slowly
into a big smile.

Part Four

Baseball Dreams and Desires

If You Have to Play Baseball

If you have to play baseball
and would much rather be home
eating a butter pecan ice cream cone
or munching on potato chips
while watching TV
or playing computer games
or even reading a book,
tell your coach your mom or dad
made you play. Say "I'd rather be
somewhere else anyway."

I bet your coach can find
something else for you to do.
After all, it's not fair
that they make you stay there
and play baseball, not fair at all
if you know a better way
to spend a summer day
than be with your friends
on a team pulling together
with the breeze kissing your face.

How the Players Felt

Hey, I got a hit!
Cool! We scored a run!
Atta girl! Katie threw a runner out at third!
Yeah! Jerome made a great diving catch!
Uh-oh. They scored the go-ahead run.
Whew! We need a rally.
Out! Man! That was a tough call.
Oh no! We lost the game.
Oh boy! Coach said we played great!

I Finally Get to Start!

I'm going to play!
Coach told me so!

I'm going to start
The game at short.

I'm batting eighth,
Right after Joe.

Boy, I can't wait
To take the court!

Oops! I mean diamond.

Baseball Card

The player's photo
on a smooth
card,

sweeter
than any
pink
stale square
of bubble gum.

All the stars
I ever
knew
mean more
to me

than all the
gum
I do not
care
to chew.

Dream Painting

Visions of home runs
color Bill's dreaming
with green thoughts,
every swing seeming
to send purple cheers
whizzing past red ears
of a blue pitcher
whose yellow tears
drop like watercolors
on the canvas
where Bill paints
his baseball dreams.

Look on the Bright Side

Ted hardly ever gets to play
   Yet comes to practice every day.
He is the nicest guy, but luck
   Just never seems to come his way.

Our uniforms are all brand new,
   An emerald green; but Ted's is blue.
The highest number's seventeen —
   Except for Ted's: it's ninety-two.

He needed large; they gave him small.
   He hardly fits in it at all.
His pants split when he bent to catch
   Coach Johnson's very first ground ball.

And in the wash the "T" (in red)
   Came off—(it changed his name to ED).
He shrugged at us and grinned. "At least
   I have a uniform," he said.

My Driveway Infield

I bounce the ball
against my garage door
and catch it on one hop
every time,
fifty times without a miss,
each bounce straight and true.

I wish I knew
why in games the ball
just won't come off
the bat
like that.

Waiting for Big

A tiny
tiny
pop fly:
it's all the
farther I
can hit.

I cannot wait
to grow
a whole lot
more
than just
a little bit.

Rain Out

On the dugout roof
raindrops thud and laugh —
they're mocking me

as
infield
rivers
wash
my
baseball
dreams
far out to sea.

Winning and Losing

Losing's as heavy
as a school lunch box
filled with mashed-
potato sandwiches.

Winning's
as
light
as a
paper
bag
bulging
with
Grandma's
fresh-
baked
caramel
corn.

The Taste of Ice Cream

Win or lose, Coach always takes us
    For a post-game treat.
"The ice cream's sour after losing.
    Winning's always sweet."

Those are the words I heard our coach,
    Mr. Johnson, say.
But as for me, I love the taste
    Of ice cream every day.

Baseball Equipment in Coach's Car

Jerry and I open coach's trunk
and see junk: golf clubs,
scattered papers, a wrench,
a pencil with a broken point,
jumper cables, two cans of oil,
a pair of golf shoes.

We also see great stuff:
a green canvas bat bag, and,
tangled amidst the jumper cables —
a greenish-brown baseball,
its scuffed cover seeming to smile
as it starts to roll
toward Jerry and me.

Here Comes Summer

Here it comes,
drying up the mud that squished
beneath our feet all spring.

Here it comes,
dotting green fields all over the land
with short-sleeved umpires yelling "Play Ball!"

Here it comes,
scattering fluffy white clouds
to keep the sun from outfielders' eyes.

Here it comes,
directing basketball, soccer and football
to move aside, to wait their turn.

There goes summer,
telling autumn to wrap baseball
in dreams to keep us warm all winter.

Home Plate's Sleeping

In winter,
home plate shivers in its sleep
under eight inches of snow.

It dreams
of batters scared,
runs scored.

It waits for melting moments,
for seasons of sunshine,
for booming bats and
the whispering whoosh
of the ump's broom.

Home plate
will awaken fast enough
when spring comes.

Batting on a Cold Day

Sometimes
my hands
sting
when I
swing
and connect.

But
even worse
is how a missed
swing
stings
my heart.

Winning Streak

Our undefeated team has got
   A mighty winning streak!
We all can hardly wait to play
   Our second game next week.

Baseball Seeds

The field is empty
except for memories
of each of us
who played here,
memories planted deep,
seeds that years from now,
after the field is parking lot
or apartment buildings,
will grow into feats
larger than all the hits
we never got, all
the plays we never made.

Star Pitcher

I throw a wicked slider;
    Another hitter whiffs.
The batters all are overmatched,
    The poor, unlucky stiffs.

In dreams I am the greatest.
    It's certainly a shame
My coach has never let me pitch
    In any baseball game.

Catcher's Gear

On a day
so hot
birds ask
for an air-conditioned
nest,

only fools,
some say,
wear tools
of ignorance:

chest protector,
shin guards,
mask.

Okay,
call me a fool,
but still
I think that
catching,
though it's hot —
is *cool*!

Waiting for the Rain

Clouds pinch away
narrow patches of blue.

By the fourth inning
gray is everywhere.

Hurry, rain. Hurry!
Wash away this game.

Wash away our opponent's
eleven runs and our strikeouts

with a cleansing downpour.
Let us be a modern day Noah

and start over.

They Always Pick Me Last

When we play baseball at recess
they always pick me last.
They never say why.
Nobody makes fun of me to my face.
They don't tell me I can't hit or catch
or that I throw and run
like somebody's eighty year old
great-grandmother.

They all seem to like me okay.
They come to my house to play.
They sit next to me at lunch.
I usually beat them all at Nintendo,
but they don't get mad at me for that.
That can't be the reason
when we play baseball at recess
no matter how many terrible players
they have to choose from
they always pick me last.

Sometimes I Lie Awake

Sometimes I lie awake
and count base hits
the way some people count sheep:

1 — a bunt down the third base line,
2 — a squibber toward first,
3 — a line drive into center,
4 — a bloop double over second,
5 — a long double in the gap,
6 — a triple high off the fence,
7 — a home run that never came down.

and because I am pitcher for our team,
I pray I'll fall asleep before I count
all the way to
10.

Part Five

A Player's Primer

With the Bat

On the Mound and On the Bases

With the Glove

Some Final Thoughts

With the Bat

The Barrel of a Bat

The barrel
of a bat
is its top,
or heavy,
part.

That's the place
to hit
the ball
to make a rally
start.

When You're Bunting

When you're bunting,
never ever
wrap your hands
around your bat.
If the ball
should hit your fingers,
something
(guess what!)
might go *splat*.

Singles and Doubles

A single
is a one-base hit;
a double
is two bases.

Batters
who get hits
like those
have laughter
on their faces.

Bunting with Two Strikes

When you bunt safely
   With two strikes
You'll make the defense scowl.

But it's a risky thing to try:
   You're out if it goes foul.

Clutch Hitter

It's fun to be called
a clutch hitter,
the one the team thinks
will come through
with "the game on the line,"
"the ducks on the pond"—
it's fun when that hitter is you.

It's fun to be called
a clutch hitter
if you've earned it
through hard work and skill.
The one who expects
to drive baserunners in
is the hitter who usually will.

Choosing the Right Bat

Make sure that your bat's
   Not too heavy or long.
If you're smart at the plate,
   You don't have to be strong.

Choke Up on the Bat

Grip that big bat on the end —
 You'll likely swing
And miss again.

But choke up on your bat a bit
 And see how well you'll
Start to hit.

Don't Argue with the Ump

Three strikes, you're out;
   Four balls, you walk;
Or else you hit the ball.

If you just stand
   And do not swing,
The umpire makes his call.

And if the ump
   Should call a strike,
Don't argue, not at all.

Contact Hitters

The more
you keep
the ball
in play,
the more
base hits
will come
your way.

How to Strike Out

Striking out
at the plate
is not hard to do.
Just swing
at every ball
pitched to you.

Don't make it
be good;
swing at everything,
and you
can be known
as a Strike Out King.

Keep Your Eyes on the Ball

Keep your eyes
on the ball
and your bat
off your shoulder,
and you'll
be a hitter
before you're much
older.

Know the Strike Zone

I've seen too many batters
    Impatient at the plate
Who haven't learned the strike zone;
    They swing when they should wait.

They swing at way-high pitches
    Above the head or neck.
They swing at those below the knees
    And make their coach a wreck.

They flail and miss, and "whiff" and "fan";
    Too often they "go down on strikes."
Those K's (a K's a strikeout)
    Are things no batter likes.

I Did It!

A home run, a homer,
A dinger, a 'tater,
A big four bagger,
A four base hit.

It happened once
On a pitch near the plate
And I swung smooth
And "got all of it."

How to Miss a Pitch

Each time
you step up
to the plate
don't close
your eyes
and swing,
for if you do,
it's likely you
will never hit
the thing!

Practice Hitting with a Tennis Ball

Practice with
a tennis ball;
Mickey Mantle did.
That's how he learned
to switch-hit
when he
was just a kid.

Hitting Foul Balls

You can hit
just as many
foul balls
as you like,

and except
for a bunt,
none can make
your third strike.

Sacrifice Bunt

Lay the bunt down,
move the runner,
and even though
you've made
an out,
you can be proud,
you've done your job;
that's what
good teamwork's
all about.

On the Mound and On the Bases

Learn to Slide the Right Way

Learn to slide the right way
   To avoid a fielder's tag.
Learn to slide the right way;
   Don't overrun the bag.

Sliding can be lots of fun;
   It covers you with dirt.
But learn to slide the right way
   So you will not get hurt.

Hook Slide

At times
it's best
to hook slide
to avoid
a fielder's
tag.

That's when
you use
your foot
to hook
the corner
of the bag.

Running to First

While running
to first
you can't
slow down
until you pass
the base.

While running
to first
you sprint sprint sprint
so you can win
the race.

Bobbles Are Part of the Game

Between pitchers
and
Teammates
Who
Make
Lots
Of
Bobbles,
there sometimes erupt
a few unpleasant squabbles.

But most pitchers know
that their teammates are trying,
and nothing good comes
out of moaning and crying.

What My Fielders Are For

I try to throw across the plate,
    For if the batter hits,
That's what my fielders are for:
    To catch it in their mitts.

Change of Pace

Zip.
Zip.
Zip.
Zip.
Whap!
That's what happens
when every pitch
comes in at identical
speed.

Zip.
Whoosh.
Ho-hum.
Whoosh.
Zip.
Vary your speeds;
a good change of pace
is what all
good pitchers
need.

Where to Run When You Hit the Ball

Of all base-running
blunders
perhaps the very
worst
is when a batter
hits the ball
then runs toward third,
not first.

Triple

You hit the ball
and run past first,
past second —
all the way to third.

You slide — you're safe!
And you've just hit
a what?
A *triple*, that's the word.

Advice to Baseball Pitchers

Don't ever pitch a spitball,
   For you would break a rule.
Don't ever pitch a spitball,
   Not even if you drool.

To pitch a spitball is an act
   I think you might regret,
Especially if it's juicy
   And gets everybody wet.

The Most Effective Pitch

A knuckler,
fast ball,
curve
and change —
of these and other types,
by far
the most effective pitch
is one
you throw for strikes.

Inside-the-Park Home Run

There's a thrilling
kind of homer,
my favorite of all:
inside-the-park,
where fielders
chase down
that bounding ball.

(It might be there's
no fence at all.)

You can't slow down,
you have to run
to get your homer.
What great fun!

Keep Your Fielders Alert

Keep walking batter
after
batter
to make your fielders
madder
and
madder.

How to Pitch a Smart Ball

Keep your eyes
on the target
as you
wind up and throw

so the ball
will remember
just where
it should go.

Bases on Balls

Pitchers
who give up
two walks
every
inning
are not
very likely
to do any
winning.

Vary the Speed

Vary the speed
   Of your pitches
So the batter can't time
   What's coming.

After you toss
   A slow, slow pitch,
Throw one that's
   Really humming!

I Never, Ever Walk

You have free passage to first base,
    When you are "hit by pitch" or walk.
So you don't have to fear or rush
    While strolling down that line of chalk.

But as for me, to reach first base
    Is quite a thrill; it's such great fun
That when I get a base on balls
    I never, ever walk. I run!

With the Glove

Back Up Bases

When you're in the field,
   Back up every throw.
Think about the places
   Every throw might go.

If a throw goes wild
   You can save the day.
Always back up bases;
   Be there to make the play.

Don't Be Nervous

Quivering and quaking
   In the field
When a ball is hit
   Your way

Isn't something
   You should do
If you want to
   Make the play.

Be a Thinking Player

Always think
a pitch
ahead
and know
just what to do

even before
the batter
swings
and hits the ball
to you.

Double Play

To get
two outs
on just
one play
will help
to make
a pitcher's
day.

When You Get Bored in the Outfield

Wear a cap with a bill as big as an awning
so your coach
and your parents
can't see that
you're yawning.

Important Positions

Of nine positions
on the field
you're sure
to have more fun
if you believe
that where *you* play's
the most
important
one.

What a Catcher Wears

Chest protector, helmet, cup.
   Two shin guards and a mask.
You need all those 'cause catching
   Can be a risky task.

You block the ball and block the plate,
   Avoid the hitter's bat.
Sometimes, with wild pitchers,
   You're like an acrobat.

Yet catching is rewarding,
   For you control the game.
And that's a role not many others
   On the field can claim.

How Not to Field a Ground Ball

Don't field a grounder
 With both your eyes shut.
Don't field a grounder
 While you're stepping back.
Don't field a grounder
 With glove turned palm down.
Don't field a grounder
 While eating a snack.

Don't field a grounder
 While standing up straight.
Don't field a grounder
 While blowing a bubble.
Don't field a grounder
 With head turned aside.
If you *do* field these ways,
 You'll have plenty of trouble.

Pull Hitters

A right-handed
pull hitter
pulls to left,
a lefty
pulls to right.
A straight-away hitter
doesn't pull much.

But be prepared,
he might.

Just Catching Them Isn't Enough

A grounder is a ball that rolls
   Or trickles on the ground.
A bouncer is a grounder
   That takes a bigger bound.

To catch those balls is only half
   Of what your job's about.
For once you make the catch, you still
   Must throw the batter out.

Grandstand Play

Some players try to show off
And make a "grandstand play"
(To make an easy catch seem hard),

But really, a far better way
To gain respect from teammates
And all the fans who watch

Is if they make the toughest play
Seem like an easy catch.

Why You Should Throw Overhanded

An overhand
throw
is more likely
to stay
much straighter
than one
thrown the sidearmed
way.

Diving for Batted Balls

When it's hit
to your side,
do you dive to catch it
or do you simply
stand
and watch it?
The players
who never
dive
I bet
see many
balls
they never get.

On a Routine Fly Ball or Pop-up, Catch the Ball with Two Hands

The only
excuse
for not using
two
is if
you have only
one
on you.

Get Your Arm Loose

Begin with easy warm-up throws
    Until your arm is loose.
Don't throw too hard too soon; your arm's
    Not made for such abuse.

Your arm is precious; warm up right
    So it will not get sore.
And though it might seem loose enough,
    Just softly toss some more.

A Catcher's Arm

It must
be accurate
and strong
for the ball
to win
the race

against
a speedy runner
who
is trying
to steal a base.

Some Final Thoughts

Baseball's Battles

A pitcher's battle is a game
   In which few runs are scored.
The pitchers battle with their arms,
   And not with shield or sword.

A hitter's battle is a game
   In which the bats are winning,
And many runners cross home plate
   In almost every inning.

And when the battle's even,
   That's when the game's most fun:
When pitchers match their goose-eggs,
   When teams match run for run.

Gopher Ball

A home run pitch
is a gopher ball,
but I really don't
know why.
The ball's
not down
in the ground at all,
but over the fence
on the fly.

Bullpen

The bullpen —
that's where pitchers throw
who might come in the game.
But no one knows exactly how
the bullpen got its name.

Some think it came
from bullfighting,
some, Indian attacks.
Some, from billboards;
some from benches
by the railroad tracks.

Its origin's a mystery,
but one thing you should know:
when you're in need
of pitching help,
The bullpen's where to go.

How Not to Treat Umps

Jaw with the umpire;
    Call him a name.
That's how to get yourself
    Tossed from the game.

How Can You Learn to Play Ball?

You can learn from a book;
   You can learn from TV.
But the best way to learn
   Is to play constantly.

You can learn from a friend,
   From a sister or brother.
You can learn from a parent
   Or even grandmother.

You can learn much from watching
   Another team play,
But the best way to learn
   Is to play every day.

Foul Line or Fair Line?

It's strange to call
a foul line foul,
for a ball that lands
on there

is not a foul ball
after all, but a ball
that's always
fair.

Managing "By the Book"

Righty versus righty;
    Lefty versus lefty:
Advantage to the pitcher.

Righty versus lefty;
    Lefty versus righty:
Advantage to the batter.

Although that precept's
    Mostly true,
Don't ever overlook

The fact that baseball's
    Always played
By people, not a "book."

Doubleheader

A doubleheader means you play
    Two ball games in a single day.
As for me, few things are better
    Than a baseball doubleheader.

Extra Base Hit

Oh, for the thrill
of an extra base hit!
Of a homer,
a triple,
or double!
For a hitter,
they're something heroic!
For a pitcher,
they're nothing but trouble.

Hustle

Always Always
Always Always
Always Always
hustle.

Doing that
can make up for
a lack of speed
or muscle.

A Coach's Signals

The third base coach
   might tug his belt
Or pinch his ear
   or touch his cap.
Those signs, or signals,
   mean as much
As any pirate's
   treasure map.

They tell the player
   when to bunt
Or when to steal or
   "take" or swing.
And when the players
   follow signs,
That's when good things
   start happening.

Baseball's treasure
   chest is full,
And thinking players
   might get rich
From the success
   that comes to those
Who know for sure
   which sign is which.

On Deck Circle

The on deck circle
   Is close to home plate.
It's where the next batter
   (Who's "on deck") must wait.

While waiting, the batter
   Should closely observe,
To study the pitcher's
   Control, speed, or curve.

For then, at the plate,
   To your happy surprise,
Whatever is pitched
   You might just recognize.

A Thankless Job

Umps — they have
   A thankless job
Calling balls
   And strikes —

Knowing they
   Can't make a call
That everybody
   Likes.

Scorebook Numbering

This scoring hint
Should help you all:
Nine numbers show
Who fields the ball.

Try to remember
The pitcher is 1;
It makes keeping score
Quite easy and fun.

His battery-mate,
The catcher, is 2.
And here are the fielders'
Numbers for you:

First base is 3
And second base, 4.
Third base is 5,
And shortstop's one more.

Left field is 7
And center is 8.
Right field is 9;
Can you keep these straight?

Baseball scorebooks
Sure look fine
With players numbered
1 through 9.

Baseball Expressions

Throwing third
to second
to first
is called
"around the horn."

A simple,
routine
fly ball?
That's easy:
"a can of corn."

Cellar Team

The cellar —
that's the bottom,
last place,
that's the
worst.

Yet many
teams,
through hard,
hard
work,
move all the way
from last
to
first.

If We Were a Major League Team

If we were a major league team,
We'd have lots of money
And draw lots of fans
And sell autographs to people
And have our pictures on bubble gum cards
And be on TV selling shoes and soda pop.

If we were a major league team,
We'd have to travel all over the country
And leave our families behind
And maybe not see them for weeks at a time,
And we'd have to sleep in strange hotels
And not have our moms here to bake us
Home-made apple pie and tuck us
In bed at night and say our prayers with us.

But we're a Little League team
And don't have to worry about how much
Money we will lose every time we strike out
Or whether we will be traded away from our friends.
We're a Little League team and no matter
Where we play we're never more
Than just a few minutes from home.
And if we make the major leagues some day,
We want to have as much fun as we do now.